BLACKBURN'S SHOPS

AT THE

TURN OF THE CENTURY

MATTHEW COLE

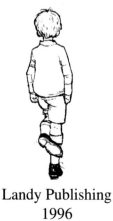

Landy Publishing
1996

> *"With care it is possible to make Blackburn a beautiful shopping centre, and attract plenty of people to traverse its streets. The people of North-East Lancashire earn good money and are good spenders."*
>
> T.P.Ritzema, owner of the *Northern Daily Telegraph*, speaking to Blackburn Chamber of Trade, November 1923.

An emblem designed by the Blackburn Chamber of Trade for the Shopping Festival of October 1921, which was intended to restore the town's status as a Mecca for consumers.

INTRODUCTION

A full generation has passed since Blackburn's town centre was transformed by the construction of the shopping precincts which now occupy it. For those whose memories stretch back to the days before anyone had heard of supermarkets, credit cards or multi-storey car parks, the town centre they first saw will have been substantially the same as that of the 1900s; but to an increasing number of Blackburn folk, that town is an historical fact, understood with difficulty from books or from the reports of their elders, rather than a personal memory.

The aim of *Blackburn's Shops at the Turn of the Century* is twofold: for those uninitiated or youthful enough to come to the town's history unsure of where fondly-talked-of landmarks and streets were, but wanting to discover more, this should help flesh out and bring to life the isolated historical facts and stories of which you may already know. For others, even aficionados of Blackburn history, there are new pictures, stories and other titbits unearthed from the records of individual shopkeepers and their customers to add to the wealth of information carefully chronicled by other local loyalists. With luck, you'll be able to find either new facts or old memories in the material here.

I am indebted to all those who have contributed something to the substance of this book, whether in the form of photographs, documents or recollections. Thanks are due to everyone who helped, but particularly to Geoff Bolton for the great benefit of his study on the subject, and to Michael Winstanley of Lancaster University for his advice. Thanks, too, to the ever-supportive and long-suffering staff of Blackburn's Central Reference Library.

Blackburn's Shops at the Turn of the Century tries to capture some of the spirit of Blackburn at the height of its trade and confidence, and to show what remains of those days. I hope it does them justice.

MATTHEW COLE
April 1996

Richard Jackson, with his young son Frank, stands proudly outside his newsagent's shop at 25, Johnston Street, which he ran from 1888-94. Although he benefited from the trade of workers in the neighbouring felt mill and chemical plant, Richard stacked his window with a dazzling display of his wares because of the fierce competition developing between shopkeepers and multiple stores, and between towns as shopping centres, at the time. Although surrounding buildings have gone, there remains a newsagent's at this address today.

SHOPPING IN BLACKBURN

Blackburn is best known to history for its industry, but the town has a longer heritage of trade. Centuries before any mill chimneys broke its skyline, Blackburn was a noted centre for buying and selling goods and services – and that tradition flourished alongside the manufacturing community of the town, prospering most with the latter's peak at the turn of the century.

A thriving market is recorded as having been run in Blackburn from the time of Queen Elizabeth I onwards. Corn, cloth and provisions were sold each Monday to local gentry and farm-bailiffs around the Market Cross where Darwen Street meets Church Street in front of the old parish church; cattle were paraded on Blakey Moor every May Day and at other regular fairs. Public proclamations such as enlistments to the army or accessions of new monarchs would be read from the steps of the Market Cross, and on special days, roasts would be held and festivities enjoyed there. Across the square, in front of where the Old Bank now stands, were the town stocks – big enough to take three culprits at a time – and even public floggings at the Cross for stealing wool were not unknown.

By the time of the industrial revolution, the compact area of under ten acres which formed the nucleus of the town was becoming very crowded. In 1774 the Monday market was replaced by two each week on Wednesday and Saturday, and new fairs had been established on Easter Monday and at Michaelmas in October. The Market Cross itself was reduced to a stump, and the old draw well was gone from the square, which was overrun by street vendors, shops, entertainers, and even traders selling 86-spindle spinning machines! Surrounding roads such as King Street were growing more and more popular as prestigious residential addresses, whilst the *'Old Bull'* pub in front of the church was the centre of riots on more than one occasion. It was increasingly clear that the facilities for trading in Blackburn were not keeping up with the prosperity of the town.

In the early Nineteenth century the town centre began to grow in response to these pressures. The new parish church was built in 1820, at which time shops first appeared on the site later known as Fleming Square, opposite the churchyard. The new road linking Blackburn with Preston joined the town centre at the top of Northgate in 1825, and from 1832 onwards, King William Street stretched out from the old Market place to that same spot, Sudell Cross. Around these modern thoroughfares sprang up imposing public buildings reflecting the new status and wealth of the town, and the pride of its leading citizens in their achievements: the

Here is the town centre, the heart of which was torn out in the redevelopment projects of the 1960s and '70s, and in which the shops in this book did business. Reproduced with permission from the 1910 Ordnance Survey Map.

railway station and market hall in 1848 (and a second market building in 1872); the Town Hall, finished in 1856; and the Cotton Exchange, begun in 1863. The Free Library and Museum opened in 1874, the foundation stone of the Technical School on Blakey Moor was laid in 1888, and last of all, the public buildings in Northgate including King George's Hall were erected between 1913 and 1921. These edifices rose up from the increasingly dense and extensive mass of houses, mills, breweries, churches, schools, shops and pubs needed to serve Blackburn's population, which multiplied more than tenfold between the early Nineteenth and Twentieth centuries. And whilst Blackburn's population doubled in the four decades to 1911, the number of retail outlets trebled. At the turn of the 20th century, an unbroken line of shops ran for a mile from the bottom of Darwen Street to Preston New Road, and a mile and a half from the Griffin to Eanam.

In particular, the nature of shops was changing, too, in tune with a developing wider industrial society. Blackburn's town centre in those days would already have had a wider variety of buildings in it than today: wholesale warehouses, selling to small-scale shopkeepers in the suburbs; mills, factories and breweries; offices, clubs, theatres, pubs and hotels in large numbers; and private homes from overcrowded and filthy rented slums to the comfortable, substantial town houses of the rich. As the Victorian era wore on, there appeared alongside the traditional businesses of individual traders or craftsmen the new phenomenon of the modern multiple chain store. In Blackburn as elsewhere, by the turn of the century, established family firms of cobblers, bakers, dressmakers, grocers, confectioners or stationers had to compete with vast organisations offering such services – sometimes various of them under one roof – in many towns, enjoying the economies of scale and American-style advertising which went with the new mass-market approach. Amongst the first was the Co-operative movement, begun in Rochdale in 1844, and of which there were 9,000 branches, by 1902, with a trade of £290,000 a year and a wholesale store in Blackburn alone. More centrally and commercially organised were famous names such as *Thomas Lipton*, whose groceries chain began in 1876, and by 1900 had seventy branches in Blackburn and around the country. *Booth's* opened their sixth shop in small premises at 40, Church Street in 1884, and moved to King William Street, where their first cafe was opened in 1902. *Marks and Spencer*, who had started business in Leeds in 1884, began their trade with the people of Blackburn from a penny bazaar in Darwen Street, but established themselves in Victoria Street as a more formidable threat to the town's own shops. *Boots the Chemists* appeared in Church Street as the new century opened, but the biggest venture of all had to await the 1930s, when *F. W. Woolworth's* magnificent Art Deco building was erected in Ainsworth Street. Across the country, the number of branches in food chains was doubling every decade after 1900, and Blackburn was touched by the same trends which brought brightly-lit, multi-storey shops employing thousands of assistants to London's Oxford Street in the first decade of this century, capitalising on the expansion not only of the population and its tastes, but also on improved transport such as the trams, and the seemingly endless stream of new innovations for the consumer, from fashionable clothes to electric lighting or flushing toilets!

'*Sod Hall*' (or sometimes '*Sod Hole*') was the engaging name given to these cottages at 303-307 Revidge Road, which were already at least a century old when this picture was taken about 1900. They were owned and rented out by the Thwaites estate, and the two shown here were run by Elizabeth Margerison as a tea shop and confectioner's. Throughout the late nineteenth and early twentieth centuries, all three cottages were shops for the growing population of Blackburn's western suburbs, and visitors who had made the trek to the top of Corporation Park.

SALESBURY, NR. BLACKBURN.

Salesbury Post Office at the corner of Ribchester Road and Lovely Hall Lane in 1908. Although the shop has gone, and the fields to the left of the picture have been built upon, the shape of the buildings seen here remains much the same today, and the *Bonny Inn*, with its beautiful views of the countryside out towards Dinckley, is still there.

These changes brought about fierce competition between shops, and there was increasingly intense price-cutting, offering of credit, flamboyant advertising and displays in shop fronts. In their defence, Blackburn shopkeepers formed a Grocers' Association in 1891, and a Tradesmen's Association in 1904, ran shopping festivals in the town, and fought for the favourable regulation of shop hours, Sunday trading, quality of goods, and even for the control of charitable ventures such as church *'Chocolate Clubs'*.

The newest and most glamourous shops, however, would often be out of reach of the pockets of ordinary Blackburn folk, who put their trust in neighbourhood shops (the trust of the shopkeeper was placed in the customer when it came to buying on tick!). Whilst in Edwardian times a High Court Judge could expect £5,000 a year, and David Lloyd George thought himself well-paid on £2,000 as President of the Board of Trade, the average man got by on around £80 a year, and poorly-paid workers such as charwomen would earn as little as £30. All in all, skilled builders, engineers or spinners in Blackburn would have up to 40s, or two pounds, for a week's work, whilst the more menial textile jobs might earn less than half of that. The Fabian Society issued a report at the time about working class family budgets entitled *Around a Pound a Week*, but in good times, a household with more than one income might see five pounds in a week.

If this seems like sparse living, remember that before 1914, a pound was worth at least £50 at today's prices. An average rent in cities outside London might be 6/6 (about 33p) per week; a full basket of groceries in Blackburn at the time came to no more than three shillings (15p). Invoices, receipts and advertisements from local shops show that at the turn of the century you could have had a shoulder of bacon for the equivalent of 19p, a pound of nutmeg for 13p, and for dessert, a dozen puddings for 38p, or a whole barrelful of apples for only 88p. Your home could be enhanced with the linoleum floor surface developed in Lancaster only a few decades earlier for a mere 7p a yard, and 41p would buy you a pegged rug to scatter over it. A man's overcoat would cost only a guinea (£1.05) in Northgate, and made-to-measure suits at *Beaty Bros.* in Church Street were reduced in the sales from £2.38 to £1.50. Less than 13p was the price of a gross of firelighters, and you could clear up the mess afterwards with a 23p stove brush - and if the fire wasn't bright enough, an attractive Marslite Globe light fitting would only set you back 6p. Best of all, the quarterly gas bill only added up to £1.30, the annual fire insurance premium (for a £200 property) was 20p, and at £1.85 for a respectable property on the Bolton Road, the rates compared favourably with today's council tax! For entertainment, in 1907 you could see the Rovers play Manchester City from a reserved seat at Ewood for 25p, or rub shoulders with Blackburn's big-wigs at the Annual Grand Conservative Ball in the Town Hall for 55p (45p for ladies).

Socially, Edwardian shops were something of a crossroads. Particularly in the smarter ones, all the affectations of a keenly class-sensitive society would be in evidence: valued middle-class patrons would be deferred to by aspiring shopkeepers, aware that though they were propertied, they were not professionals. Below them were the assistants whose work (although they might consider themselves 'better'

13

This imposing building is Blackburn's Vicarage, which stood at the corner of *King Street* and *Freckleton Street* in 1906, when this photograph was first published.It illustrates the variety of buildings - private homes, factories, offices, warehouses, churches, theatres and clubs - with which Blackburn's shops had to compete for space at the turn of the century.

than industrial workers) was poorly-paid, and often involved long hours, short holidays, fines for minor offences, few prospects of promotion, and *'living in'* amidst dirty and cramped quarters, conditions which gave rise to a Government Commission and several Shop Acts at the time. Along with the more personal and relaxed style of the corner shop or family grocer went the falsely genteel and obsequious social world of H.G. Wells' *History of Mr. Polly* (1910) or *Kipps* (1905), in which one shopman says: *"I tell you we're in a blessed drainpipe and we've got to crawl along it till we die"*. Figures from the Trade Union Congress showed numbers of girls working up to 100 hours a week for a few shillings, and as many as 700 Blackburn shops opened on Sundays, too.

For all that, in a middle-sized town like Blackburn, shops were one of the places in a locality where people of varied backgrounds would most regularly meet: they would discuss events national and local, private and public, sporting, social and political, in a more congenial atmosphere than the age of the checkout and self-service allows. The busy days would be different when Blackburn factory girls only got a morning off for Christmas shopping, but the town closed altogether for the Wakes holidays. For Blackburn's shoppers at the turn of the century, even mundane shopping could be a pleasure as well as a duty, and a look at the places, people and products involved can tell us a great deal.

FLEMING SQUARE

Fleming Square was Blackburn's first purpose-built shopping mall. It was built in the early 1820s by John Fleming, a successful textile merchant who was appointed a trustee for the rebuilding of the Parish Church in 1819. Legend has it that the new square, built on the former site of the town's fish-stones and running alongside the old cloth hall, was made of masonry taken from the old church across Darwen Street, and whilst this part of the story now seems unlikely, the legendary prosperity of the project is beyond dispute. As early as 1824 the premises, consisting of a tiered building with an iron-colonnaded front, surrounded by terraces of shops and pubs, boasted nearly fifty separate businesses, half of them butchers continuing the trade in food previously carried on at the site. In the mid-Victorian era, Fleming's Square was a busy and varied thoroughfare: it hosted the offices of the Blackburn Mail, and the first meetings of the prestigious *'Union Club'*, and one of its garrets provided a home in 1853 for John C. Prince, the *'reedmaker poet'* who became one of Blackburn's most noted writers. One large room was even rented out for dramatic performances, although these were makeshift affairs, and one, 'Rob Roy', produced without stage or scenery, met with such coarse impudence from the unseated and motley audience that they were whipped from the building by the leading actor! Fleming, who lived nearby in Clayton Street, and later King Street, died in 1842, but his property venture lived on: in 1849 the *'Exchange Arcade'* was added, and still bears what is said to be Fleming's likeness above the datestone. Two years later, Whittle wrote of the Square that it did its architect *"infinite credit, and at the same time adds to the beauty and respectability of the town"*. It certainly accommodated a diverse range of occupants, including over the following century, tin and iron workshops, upholsterers and drapers, French polishers and printers, insurance brokers, couriers and banks, a Spiritualist church, working men's institutes, the Trade Defence Association, the Conservative registration office, and the Girl Guides' headquarters! The Exchange Arcade even housed a hot-air bath built by former handloom weaver George Hopwood, who also ran his own mill and a dancing school at Tockholes exclusively for 'navvies' from Withnell water works! Many of these traders stayed in the Square for decades, and most were operating at the turn of the century, but by Edwardian times other parts of town were stealing Fleming Square's erstwhile glamour. In 1877 William Abram regretted that it was *"once a busy mart, but now comparatively forsaken"*; William Hulme and J.G.Shaw warned more bluntly in 1889 that *"it is a foretaste of martyrdom for anyone to be compelled*

Fleming Square, captured in 1947, when it looked much as it had for a century, by local artist Edmund Mercer. He now works on Whalley Banks as a printer and publisher of art and poetry.

OLD BLACKBURN.
FLEMING SQUARE
EDMUND MERCER/47.

The lobby of the *Castle Hotel*, Market Street Lane, as illustrated in an advert of 1896. The meeting place of Blackburn's business community, it was rebuilt in 1893 in a style befitting its name. The Castle was a cut above some of the neighbouring pubs, and admission was refused to those without jacket and tie.

THE PRINCIPAL STAIRCASE

16

Telephone 1401   16, 18 & 20. Fleming Square. BLACKBURN, AUG 4- 1905 19

SPECIALITIES.
ABC SELF RAISING FLOUR.
BAKING POWDER.
EGG POWDER.
CUSTARD POWDER.
HEALTH SALT
FURNITURE CREAM.
&c.

IMPORTERS OF
DRIED FRUIT
RICE SPICE
SEEDS and OILS

Marrowfat Peas
a speciality.

BOUGHT OF

POMFRET BROTHERS.

Pomfret Bros. was one of the shops which used to face the Exchange Arcade on the now empty groung behind Lloyds Bank. The firm prospered for half a century, at its height, as here, occupying three houses. Pomfrets' receipts also reflect grocers' concern over accusations of food adulteration at the turn of the century, with the boast *"all peppers and spices sold by us guaranteed pure"*.

THE BLACKBURN BANK, LIMITED.
LOAN DEPARTMENT.
Advances (strictly private) made in town or country. House holders (male or female), Farmers, Tradesmen, and others on easy terms. Repayments to suit the convenience of borrowers. For terms apply to the Manager, 9 and 11, Fleming-square, Blackburn, or   THOS. DOBSON, Agent, 23, Warner-street, Accrington.

Blackburn Bank gave loans from the two units in Exchange Arcade nearest Darwen Street. This advert dates from August 1889, but the bank had gone by the early twentieth century.

Swarbrick's and **Parker's** stood right alongside Pomfret's on the north side of the Square, and demonstrate the enduring and varied nature of the shops there. Workshops dealing in metals did business beside offices, tailors and pubs; Elizabeth Swarbrick served provisions amid this tumult for nearly fifty years.

8, FLEMING SQUARE, OCT 10 189?.
Blackburn,
Mr J Bolton
Bought of E. SWARBRICK,
WHOLESALE PROVISION MERCHANT.
IMPORTER OF IRISH, AMERICAN AND CONTINENTAL PRODUCE. HOME-CURED HAMS AND BACON.
TERMS : CASH ; LESS 4D. IN 14 DAYS ; 3D. MONTH ; EGGS STRICTLY CASH IN 7 DAYS.
Interest charged on overdue Accounts.

10 FLEMING SQUARE, Nov 28 1892.
BLACKBURN,
Mr J. Bolton
BOUGHT OF C. PARKER,
Wholesale Iron and Tin-plate Worker,
AND GENERAL HARDWARE FACTOR.
NETT. ACCOUNTS MONTHLY.

to walk through this villainously-paved place of cobble stones and cellar openings". By 1906 there were only 22 shops and offices there, and barely a dozen remained by the time of the Second World War. Most of the buildings around the Square were demolished during the developments of the 1960s, to make way for modern replacements or open spaces. Only the Arcade and the pillared facade of this once bustling shoppers' haunt remain to remind us of its former glory.

Above: **John Critchley Prince** (1808-1866), the *'reed-maker poet'*, who was part of the colourful life of **Fleming Square** whilst he lived there during the 1850s. A renowned drinker and debtor, and a political radical, it was said of Prince by one of his creditors that he *'wrote like an angel, and lived like a devil'*.

Right, and elsewhere in this book: Here we see a copy of a page from the Barrett's Directory for 1897 which shows who was living or working at the various premises in Fleming Square. A page is reproduced for each location in this book.

U.M.F. Church
Paradise lane
11 & 13 Greenwood W.,
  baths
15 Warburton J., ice
  cream maker
17 Wensley R., smith (j.)
19 Balshaw J., mechanic
21 Hampson R., carter
23 Sunderland Mrs. E.
25 Kirtlan B., joiner (j.)
27 Balshaw Miss A.,dress-
  maker
29 Reid Miss M. A., shop-
  keeper
31 Rostron Mrs. E.
33 Hayes R., police con
35 McDonald J., pol con
37 Robinson W., chair-
  maker (j.)
39 Heim J., fried fish dlr
41 Walker A., clerk
43 Kirtlan Mrs. Eliz.
45 Duxbury W. H., hard-
  ware dealer
47 Rawlinson T., bailiff
49 Littler A., butcher
Princes street
51 Caton J., joiner
53 Aaron I., picture frmr
55 Tattersall Mrs. A.
57 Halliday D., joiner (j.)
Montague street
80 Hill H. T., coachman
78 Cleminson Mrs. M. E.,
  registry office
76 Barber W., coachbldr
74 Loynds Mrs. M. A.,
Prince Albert
72 Kay Mrs. Elizabeth
70 Kay J. G., hairdresser
66 & 68 Cheetham J.,
  grocer
Bradshaw street
64 Duxbury A., stationer
62 Dean T., moulder
60 Frankham J., bootmkr
58 Dean R., spinner
56 Hyslop D., moulder
54 Long Mrs. Mary
52 Robinson G., musician
50 Grimshaw J., fruiterer
48 Baines & Holland
  (Misses)
46 Leeming Mrs. A.
44 Featherstone W. T.,
  police constable
42 Redfern R., mason (j.)
40 French Mrs. Alice
36 Child Mrs. Harriet
34 Duxbury W.H.,clothes
  dealer
32 Panter Mrs. J., clothes
  dealer

30 Fort W., grocer
Bond street
28 Haworth J., grocer
26 Blackburn Mrs. A.,
  draper
24 Harris T., chairmaker
22 Mayo W., tailor
20 Laxton A., chapel kpr
18 Higson D., herbalist
16 Brunskill W., ropemkr
14 Dowse G. A., grocer
Warwick street
10 & 12 Dugdale T., boot-
  maker
8 Hayhurst J., brewr (j.)
6 Baron Mrs. Elizabeth
4 Waddington T., carter
2 Coupe R. W., optician

FECITT BROW.

Hargreaves B., farmer,
  Shadsworth
Holden Jas., *Foresters'
  Arms*
Naisby T., carter
14 Mullineaux J., jnr (j.)
10 Parsons Mr. Charles
8 Brindle T., miner
6 Gouldsbrough T., wvr
Riley J., *Fountain Inn*

FERGUSON ST.,
EWOOD.

1 Haworth T., mason (j.)
3 Wiggins W., eng tenter
5 Graham J., watchman
14 Allen G., weaver
10 McCann G. H., spinnr
6 Mather A., paper mkr
2 Robinson A., weaver

FERNHURST ST.,
LIVESEY.

7 Holden J., jobber
9 Slater E., clerk
11 Walmsley W. H.,
  bookkeeper
13 Whittaker T., stoker
15 Eatough Jno., schlmstr
17 Hoskinson H., fireman
21 Shaw G., fireman
Conlong J., mechanic
Heys W. H., clothlkr
Jackson T., weaver
Turner T., weaver

FISHER STREET.

23 Sutton W., chim swpr
26 St. Anne's Co-op. stores
Swarbrick street
Leeming R. & Sons,
  shuttle manufactrs

87 Mercer J.T.,watchmkr
97 Brandwood W., shpkpr
103 Walne J., signalman
112 Gorner J., watch repr
70 Weaver T., grocer

FISH MARKET.

Baines T., fishmonger
Connor Mrs. C., fish-
  monger
Duckworth E.,fishmgr
Tomlinson W., fishmgr
WhalleyW.H.,fishmgr
Kennedy T. & S.,
  oyster dealers
Wardhaugh F., game
  dealer

FLEMING SQ.

1 & 3 Hamer R. & Sons,
  ironmongers
9 & 11 Blackburn Bank,
  Ltd.; R. Shorrock,
  manager
13 & 15 Hopwood G., baths
17, 19, & 21 Davies R. &
  Son, engineers
31 Parkinson T., bootmkr
33 and 61 Maguire &
  Richards, drysalters
59 Jennings J., tinner
Eaves & Sharples,
  pattern makers
67 Cooke R., bootmaker
69 Sergeant W. L., gun-
  maker
73 Pace A., sign writer
75 Parkinson R., painter
22 Higham J. H. & R. T.,
  wholesale grocers
20 & 18 Pomfret Bros.,
  wholesale druggists
18aConservative Registra-
  tion Office; E. Holt
14 Proctor W. H., leather
  dealer
12 Jepson R., paper hang-
  ings merchant
10 Parker J. & Co., tinners
8 Swarbrick Mrs. E.,
  provision merchant
6 Bowker Mrs. A., *Edin-
  burgh Hotel*

FLORENCE ST.

Clifton & Kersley Coal
  Co., Limited; W.
  Grainger, agent
9 Kenyon Mrs. Ann
11 Haworth J., quarrymn
13 Wadsworth Miss Ellen

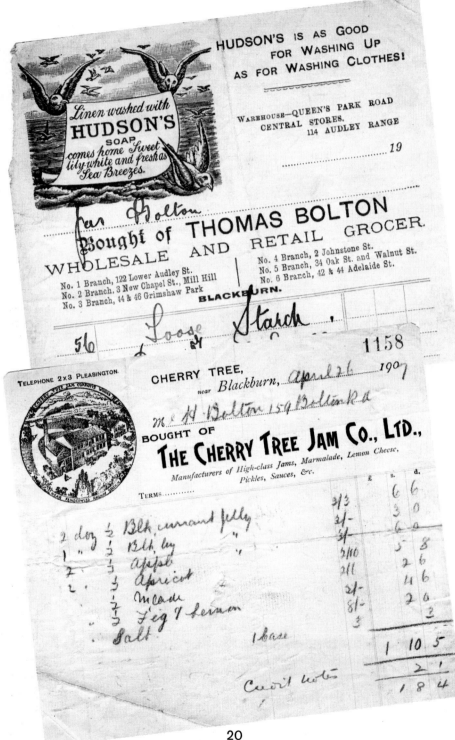

HUDSON'S IS AS GOOD
FOR WASHING UP
AS FOR WASHING CLOTHES!

Linen washed with
HUDSON'S
SOAP
comes home Sweet
lily-white and fresh as
Sea Breezes.

WAREHOUSE—QUEEN'S PARK ROAD
CENTRAL STORES.
114 AUDLEY RANGE

.... 19

Bought of THOMAS BOLTON
WHOLESALE AND RETAIL GROCER.

No. 1 Branch, 122 Lower Audley St.
No. 2 Branch, 3 New Chapel St., Mill Hill
No. 3 Branch, 44 & 46 Grimshaw Park

No. 4 Branch, 2 Johnstone St.
No. 5 Branch, 34 Oak St. and Walnut St.
No. 6 Branch, 42 & 44 Adelaide St.

BLACKBURN.

56   1 Loose Starch   1158

TELEPHONE 2 x 3 PLEASINGTON.

CHERRY TREE,
near Blackburn, *April 26 1907*

M. H. Bolton 159 Bolton Rd

BOUGHT OF
THE CHERRY TREE JAM CO., LTD.,

Manufacturers of High-class Jams, Marmalade, Lemon Cheese,
Pickles, Sauces, &c.

TERMS...........

	£	s.	d.
2 doz ½ Blk. currant jelly	3/3	6	6
1 " ½ Blk. by	3/-	3	0
2 " ½ Apple	3/-	6	0
2 " ½ apricot	2/10	5	8
" ½ meade	2/11	2	6
" Fig & lemon	2/-	4	6
" Salt	8/-	2	0
1 case	3		3
		1 10	5
Credit notes		2	1
		1 8	4

20

NORTHGATE

Northgate is one of Blackburn's oldest thoroughfares. Before Elizabethan times it was one of the four arms of the crossroads which met in the old market-place at the junction with Darwen Street, Church Street and Astley Gate. Originally, Northgate ran from where the *'Sun Inn'* stands in Astley Gate, straight through Limbrick, up Shear Brow and out of town. Such an important route to market naturally became a popular site for trade, and by the 1820s, there were already eight shops, pubs and workshops doing business in Northgate, including everything from cabinet makers and earthenware dealers to milliners, cloggers, hosiers, tailors and grocers, butchers, bakers, and - quite literally - candlestick-makers, or tallow chandlers, as they were known. Some Northgate shopkeepers, like draper Richard Haworth, went on to become major players in the Blackburn textile business. At least ten of these men were local Freeholders, and a further half-dozen of this propertied class lived in neighbouring Astley Gate or Blakey Moor - in all, nearly one in ten of the town's total.

The Northgate area also had a reputation for its robust social life. The road boasted fifteen pubs throughout the Nineteenth century, as well as wine stores, many with rented rooms and stables to cater for those in the textile trade travelling in to market. In 1824, this represented almost one fifth of all the pubs in Blackburn. Amongst the better known was the *'Paganini Inn'* on the Southern corner of Northgate and Higher Cockcroft: previously known as the *'Joiner's Arms'*, it had been serving Blackburn drinkers since before the reign of George III, but changed title to mark the performance in the town of the renowned Italian violin virtuoso Nicolo Paganini on September 5th, 1833, when he stayed at the pub. His sleep was reputedly interrupted by the discovery of a large rodent in the bed which drove the maestro to wander up and down Nothgate until dawn. The Paganini survived until 1899, when it was closed by local temperance activists, who had their own hotel in Northgate. Musical entertainment was also the theme at the *'King's Arms'* the other side of Higher Cockcroft, where a Gentlemen's Glee Club was founded in 1849. A few doors away in Lower Cockcroft, the *'Prince of Wales Club'* – whose Fleur-de-Lys design can still be seen in the windows of the commercial premises now occupying the building – was probably the venue for more illicit pursuits, as a secret tunnel connected the interior with Barton Street. The entertainment may have been cockfighting, since an Eighteenth-century document, as well as the streetnames, point to Northgate as the site of the local cockpit. Along with drink and gaming

NORTHGATE.

1 and 3 Tills, clothiers
7 Pye A., ironmonger
9 Ainsworth J., jeweller
11 Charnley J. T., tailor
Lord Street west
11aHarris S., draper
13 Keir J. M., cycle mnfr
15 Stubbs, Limited, mercantile offices
17 Allan J., optician
19 Whiteside W., bootmkr
Lower Cockcroft
Lomax, Limited, door furniture makers
Farmery J. & Son, printers
21 and 23 Mercer Bros., ironmongers
25 Fairbrother C. H., pork butcher
27 Moore R., draper
29 Taylor Mrs. J., *Paganini Inn*
Higher Cockcroft
9 Wilding R., pudding maker
31 Fairbrother C. H., *King's Arms*
33 Clarkson J., pawnbrkr
35 Cottam W. H., *Ribblesdale Hotel*
New Market Street west
35aFederation of Horsemen; G.W. Pickard, secretary
37 Bramwell J. T., hairdresser
39 Crossland H. S., cutler
41 Cockshott T., *Black Horse Inn*
43 Dewhurst J., clogger
Engine street
45 Wienburg I., tailor
47 Leaver J. & Son, pntrs
49 Airey F., plumber
51 Weall J. B., *Dairy Cows Inn*
Cannon street
53 Parkinson Mrs. E., *Devonshire Hotel*
55 Hayhurst W., *Red Lion Hotel*
57 Taylor J., shopkeeper
59 Coop H., broker
Queen street
61 Cunliffe J., grocer
63 Bramwell C., hairdrsr
65 Sames & Green, archts
65 *Deaf and Dumb Institute;* W. H. F. Sames, hon sec
67 Garsden W., butcher

69 Aspden Mrs. P., *General Wolfe Inn*
71 Sowerbutts W., grocer
Duke street
73 Briggs T., printer
75 Cooper E., solicitor
77 Woods G. H. & Co., electrical engineers
79 Pomfret R., rope mnfr
81 Pomfret R., draper
Sudell cross
108 Cook J. W., *Grapes Inn*
Whiteside R., hay dlr
104 Ramsbottom J., sign writer
102 Davenport E. J., prntr
100 McCabe J., shoemaker
98 Caton H., baker
96 Dean R., upholsterer
92 Butler C., watchmaker
Town Hall street
90 Kinghorn Percy, *Masons' Arms*
88 Shaw & Porter, sadlrs
86 Brewer J., chemist
Spencer J., smith
Spencer T., wheelwght
80 Fielding R. A., grocer
78 Shaw R., stationer
76 Booth Mrs. E. M., drpr
74 Metcalfe & Sons, bootmakers
70 Fowler T., spirit mcht
68 Pickup H., painter
68aBrooks B., hairdresser
Back New Market street
Clark J., cabt mkr
64 Arkwright F., provision merchant
62 and 60 Fish P., *George and Dragon*
New Market street
56 & 58 Ditchfield R. T., tailor
54 Parkinson J., provision merchant
52 Butler T., hosier
48 Walker Eli, tailor
44 and 46 Margerison L., *Nag's Head*
42 Kelly H. & Co., leather dealers
40 Mitchell S. & J., dealers in photo apparatus
36 and 38 Mitchell J., *Alliance and Commercial Hotel*
34 Widdup J., tobaccnst
24 Woods W. H., printer
20 Dearden G., *Stanley Arms*
18 Bradley W., cycle dlr
Lord street
14 Hargreaves J., draper

12 Ellidge J., clothier
8 & 10 Linaker Mrs. C., baby linen dealer
4 Walsh Mrs. S. E., confectioner
2 Sharples H. & Son, music sellers

NOTTINGHAM ST.

4 Derbyshire J., weaver
8 Bury V., manager
10 Yates Mrs. M.
12 Hague T., shoemkr (j.)
14 Hopper J. T., drawr-in
16 Houghton J., weaver
20 Grimshaw Mrs. B.
30 Haydock R., overlkr
36 Bleasdale Mr. J.
40 Morris W., overlooker
44 Piercy R. S., millwrght
46 Edmondson W., clthlkr
48 Smith H., spinner
54 Benson J., police cons
58 Brindle E., overlooker
60 Prescott J., taper
62 Newby Geo., mason (j.)
64 Payne W., moulder
66 Carter W., weaver
70 Duckworth J., weaver

NUTTALL STREET.

110 Tillotson Soap Co.
112 Fallows J. H., mchnc
118 Ainsworth A., clerk
130 Calvert R., eng driver
134 Fell R., weaver
140 Dowbakin T., weaver

OAK STREET.

1 Barker T., joiner (j.)
23 Wignall Miss Martha
29 Higham E., cabinet maker (j.)
34 Bolton J., grocer
Read & Sharples, Oozeboth mill

OLD CHAPEL ST.

1 Holt T., shopkeeper
3 Gilbert W., broker
5 Killeen Mrs. Mary
7 Padley R., upholsterer
9 Cross J., *Boar's Head*
11 & 13 Waring W., marine store dealer
15 Walker E., greengrcr
14 & 16 Billington T., *Regent Hotel*
Water street
14 Whittaker M., shpkpr
12 Moore E., shopman

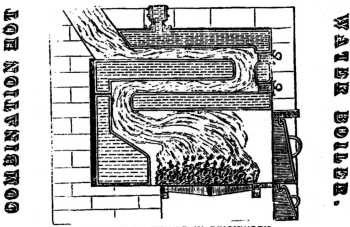
Mercer's Ironmongers is the great survivor of Blackburn shops. The family firm has been offering a wide variety of goods from its Northgate premises since 1840, as this advert from a nineteenth century directory shows.

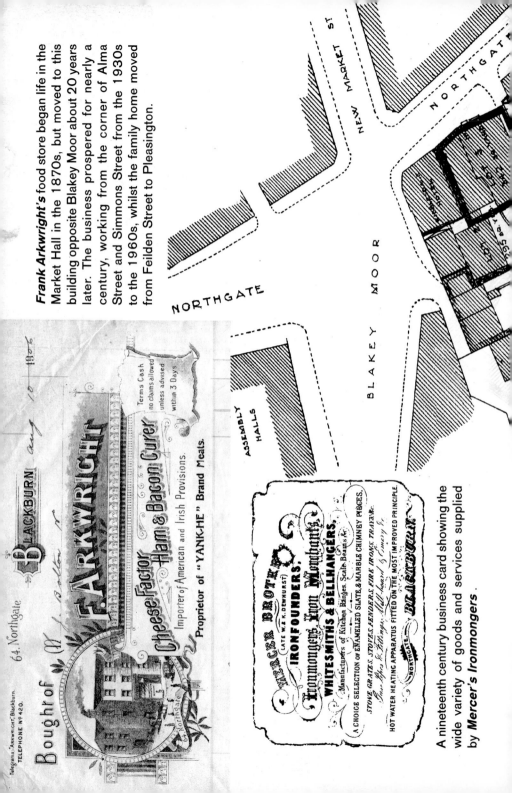

Frank Arkwright's food store began life in the Market Hall in the 1870s, but moved to this building opposite Blakey Moor about 20 years later. The business prospered for nearly a century, working from the corner of Alma Street and Simmons Street from the 1930s to the 1960s, whilst the family home moved from Feilden Street to Pleasington.

NORTHGATE

NEW MARKET ST

NORTHGATE

BLAKEY MOOR

ASSEMBLY HALLS

Telegrams-"Arkwright" Blackburn.
TELEPHONE Nº 420.

BLACKBURN Aug 10 1906

Bought of

64. Northgate.

F. ARKWRIGHT

Cheese Factor

Ham & Bacon Curer

Importer of American and Irish Provisions.

Proprietor of "YANK-HE" Brand Meats.

Terms Cash
no claims allowed
unless advised
within 3 Days

MERCER BROTHE
(LATE W.F.K. DEWHURST)

IRONFOUNDERS,

Ironmongers, Iron Merchants,

WHITESMITHS & BELLHANGERS,

Manufacturers of Kitchen Ranges, Scale Beams &c.

A CHOICE SELECTION OF ENAMELLED SLATE, & MARBLE CHIMNEY PIECES,

STOVE GRATES, STOVES, FENDERS, FIRE IRONS, TRAYS &c.

HOT WATER HEATING APPARATUS FITTED ON THE MOST IMPROVED PRINCIPLE.

BLACKBURN

Gas & Hot Water Fittings. Well-boxed by Emery St.

A nineteenth century business card showing the wide variety of goods and services supplied by *Mercer's Ironmongers*.

Northgate in 1927. This surveyor's map shows the streets surrounding Blakey Moor when King George's Hall was only 15 years old, and shops, pubs and workshops stretched all the way back to Barton Street.

The Peel Hotel was not the only hostelry to take the name of the famous Blackburn family, but its address on the corner of Barton Street and Cardwell Place, facing the birthplace of the first Sir Robert Peel, father of the Prime Minister, gave it distinction. Open since the early 1870s, it now looks rather different, having lost its name and adjoining cottage.

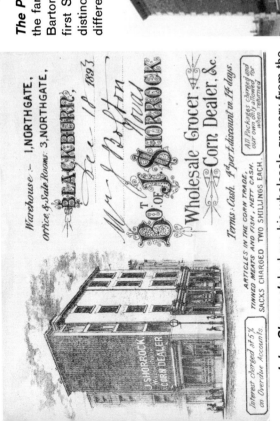

John Shorrock had run his wholesale grocery from the corner of Northgate and Astley Gate for twelve years when this receipt was issued in 1893. Within another three years, the firm moved to Mincing Lane, and opened a warehouse in Clayton Street. This building was pulled down to make way for the new car park in the 1960s.

came occasional disturbances: in 1828, soldiers from the 67th Regiment of Foot (who had earned a reputation for brutality in Blackburn) clashed with local men, women and children in a running battle down Northgate and into Fleming Square, near their King Street barracks. The Cotton Famine of 1862 saw an attempt to rescue four men convicted of poaching to feed their families, during which 200 Special Constables were called in to control crowds, and the Riot Act was read in Northgate. As late as 1891, Northgate was noted by the *Blackburn Times* as one of Blackburn's roughest areas, where pubs were *"as common as blackberries on a hedge"*; Blakey Moor generally was condemned at the time as a *"mass of poor and squalid property. It abounds in tramps' lodgings and houses of an even worse description"*.

Indeed, by the Edwardian period, Northgate had lost much of its prestige, even if it remained busy. In 1910, seventy businesses of very varied character still ran there, but the most expensive and fastest-growing shops were elsewhere in the town. Northgate had been bisected by Preston New Road in 1824, creating the flourishing sites of King William Street and Sudell Cross; in 1912, the erection of the public halls and police station obliterated Queen Street and Cannon Street to the West; other shops were later replaced by the Co-operative store, now the Central Library. Post-war developments sectioned off the old road to the market at Limbrick in the North, and Astley Gate at the bottom, and raised the shopping centre which ensured that Northgate, once the most vibrant of Blackburn's streets, became little more than a side road stringing together other junctions and turnings. A last memory of the old Northgate stands at No.21, where *Mercer's* ironmongers has been in business since 1840, in a building proudly decorated with stone lions' heads, and dating back at least to 1825. The Mercer family not only sold and serviced heating systems, but also for a time in the late Nineteenth century made boilers at a foundry in Eagle Street. At the turn of the century, they met competition from half-a-dozen ironmongers in Northgate by opening from six in the morning until ten at night and boasted hundreds of patrons amongst schools, clubs, banks, churches and even the private home of Lord Cecil as far afield as Morecambe and Dorsetshire. Some time after the War, twenty pairs of Mercer's men were still working full-time on site at mills in Blackburn using the firm's systems. Now, the mills and the old surroundings of Northgate have vanished, Mercer's has had to adapt to survive.

Left: The coronation of Edward VII in August 1902 was celebrated at the *Devonshire Hotel* in *Northgate* with best suits, billowing flags and a banner proclaiming '*May Our Town and Trade Flourish*'! The Devonshire was one of more than fifteen pubs in Northgate at the turn of the century, and stood at the corner of Cannon Street. By the end of Edward's reign in 1910, the building had become the Public Health Office, and was about to be demolished to make way for the Police Station and King George's Hall.

Glober,

Hatter.

Shirts

Made to Order.

Collars

Made to Pattern.

Globes A Speciality.

Hosier, Outfitter.

All Ladies' and Gent.'s Globes fitted on before purchasing.

Specialist in Ladies' and Gent.'s Hosiery.

WILLIAM WILSON,
6, HIGHER CHURCH ST., BLACKBURN.

GENTLEMEN!

Have you seen our stock of

HATS AND CAPS?

If not,

William Wilson had a hat and glove shop just above Lloyd's Bank in *Higher Church Street* for a quarter of a century before the First World War, and lived at addresses in London Road, St. Andrew's Street off Limbrick, and Wellington Street, St. John's. The well-stocked window with its ornate lamps is not recognisable today, because the building, a crumbling patchwork of different generations' masonry, was given a new brick face in 1985. However, the interior still has rushwork in the roof, and shows evidence of the days when the shop served its original purpose as two separate cottages.

CHURCH STREET

SALFORD

Church Street is not only one of Blackburn's oldest shopping haunts, but also its most prestigious. As the Eastern arm of the crossroads in the Market Square, Church Street has always been at the centre of local trading activity, but in addition it has been the address of a number of splendid and significant buildings. A little over a century ago, Shaw and Hulme wrote that *"we have not much architecture to boast of in Blackburn, but the symmetry of the blocks of lofty new buildings around Salford Bridge is really remarkable, and a credit both to the architects who have designed them and the businessmen who have invested their money"*.

Salford Bridge – now virtually smothered by surrounding roads – was the meeting point of some of the most important routes into Blackburn. Standing at it a century ago, you would have looked one way towards Eanam into the factories, mills and breweries that generated Blackburn's wealth; in the other direction, up Church Street, were the addresses of the institutions which were the pillars of respectable Blackburn society. All around the spot, busy streets of shops, warehouses and offices now gone in all but name – such as Ainsworth Street, Penny Street and Victoria Street – stretched away.

Apart from the church itself, completely rebuilt in its current gothic grandeur in the 1820s, Nineteenth-century Church Street had the town's post office, and later acquired its banks, most notably the *'Old Bank'* still standing at the corner with Darwen street. Built in 1878 in a striking style symbolic of the self-confidence of Blackburn's financial guardians, the Old Bank was commended thirty years ago in Pevsner's *'The Buildings of England'* as *"one of the best buildings in Blackburn"*. Alongside these were some of Blackburn's best-loved and longest-established public houses, including the *'Bay Horse'* and *'White Bull'*, facing each other across Salford Bridge, the *'George & Dragon'* and the *'Old Bull'*, rebuilt in 1847, which faced the old market-place and backed onto the churchyard, and was the scene in alternate days and weeks of business meetings amongst textile barons, and riots by political radicals and loom-breakers. Over the grand entrance to *'Thwaites' Arcade'* were the offices of the Conservative Party, many of whose most influential and active supporters – including Blackburn's two MPs – would also gather at the *'Union Club'*, 9 & 11 Higher Church Street. Terraces of Victorian houses-turned-shops huddled around newer and bigger premises such as the offices of the *Evening Post*, or, around the corner in Ainsworth Street, the *'Theatre Royal'*.

The considerable traffic attracted by these enterprises, especially the railway

The *Union Club*, left, stood in *Higher Church Street*, opposite the Old Bank, and had originally been built for Henry Sudell upon his marriage in 1786. Between 1853 and 1922, the club entertained Blackburn's social elite - four of its Chairmen were local MPs.

129, Penny Street,
Blackburn. *Dec 27* 1888

M Bolton Norris

Bought of WILLIAM ALMOND,
WHOLESALE
Potato Dealer & Provision Merchant.

Dec 93
| 10 |
| 9 ½ |
| 9 ½ |
| 10 ¼ |
| 11 ¾ |
| 10 ¾ |
| 61 - ½ lbs at 9 | 2 | 6 ½ |

Thomas Coupe & Co. sold tea and coffee from premises in *Ainsworth Street* from the 1880s to the 1960s, having moved from Mincing Lane and Corporation Street. The grand building shown here is No.29, and stood roughly where the newest shop developments have recently been made facing the market complex.

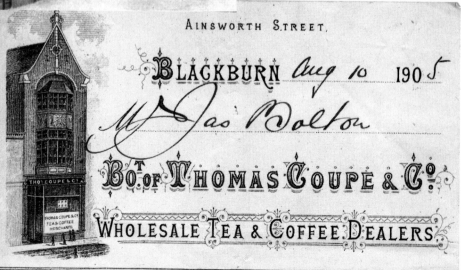

AINSWORTH STREET,

BLACKBURN *Aug 10* 1905

M Jas Bolton

Bo.of THOMAS COUPE & Co.

WHOLESALE TEA & COFFEE DEALERS,

Telephone 0954.

New Water Street,

BLACKBURN, *Oct. 31 1906*

Mr *James Bolton.*

BOUGHT OF

HOLDEN & Cº.

Wholesale Tea & Coffee Blenders,

TO THE TRADE.

ALL CUSTOMERS' TEAS HELD BY US ARE PROTECTED FROM LOSS BY FIRE.

INTEREST AT THE RATE OF 5% PER ANNUM CHARGED ON OVERDUE ACCOUNTS.

Terms 1 Month Prompt.

New Market Street ran alongside the River Blakewater under the current site of the Market front at Salford Bridge. *Holden & Co.* was one of several large wholesale tea warehouses in the town centre.

Church Street, seen here from either end in two postcards of 1907 and 1909, now has only the buildings seen on the south side.

The French visitor who sent the cards to his family in Versailles complained that "the weather is so cold it pinches me!"

after the station opened in 1848, made Church Street one of the first parts of Blackburn to be redeveloped. Salford Bridge in particular became a bottle-neck of horses, carts and pedestrians, crowded with property, and – despite its inoffensive name, meaning *'safe' or 'sallow' ford* – was periodically flooded by the River Blakewater. The bridge was widened first with the opening of Railway (then Station) Road in the 1840s, when the Blakewater was diverted away from the road, and again in 1882, when the streets around the bridge were doubled or trebled in size, and three feet were shorn off the hump in the bridge. Slums were demolished and hotels lavishly rebuilt under special Acts of Parliament, and traffic islands were added to give Edwardian Church Street the impression of a cosmopolitan boulevard as much as the heart of a world industrial centre.

In this area perhaps as much as anywhere in Blackburn, developments in living memory have done most to obliterate the evidence of the past. Both the glamour of Thwaites' Arcade and the grubbiness of the stagnant Blakewater were swept away in the construction of the existing market and shopping centre, rendering titles such as *'Bridge'* and *'Street'* virtual misnomers, and turning Salford itself into little more than a junction. Here more than anywhere else, it is difficult for those who did not witness it even to picture the view, or conceive of the basic street plan around Church Street, as it was until the 1960s.

BOYLES' CLOTHES SHOP

When first I came into the town
I found that cloth was bad;
But very soon I let them see
Where good stuff could be had.
Having a knowledge of the trade,
Likewise the price of clothes;
I soon got into a shop of my own
As everybody knows.

Chorus–

So if you want a suit of clothes,
Just come up to me;
I have all sorts and sizes,
And with them you can make free.
My place is top of Penny Street,
Painted up on the top,
Seventy-four, Seventy-six.
Boyles' Clothes Shop.

The father of eight bouncing sons
Strongly does advise
All parents for to send their sons,
No matter what their size.
Tom Thumb gave me an order once,
And a giant seven feet;
They made the long and short of it,
At my Shop in Penny Street.

Chorus–

So if you want a suit of clothes, &c.

Two gentlemen came into my shop,
Each wanted a suit;
I thought my money was all safe,
For I did like their look.
One he was a working man
With any amount of brass;
The other he seemed light-hearted,
For he said he worked at the Gas.

Chorus–

So if you want a suit of clothes, &c.

I've suits for men, and suits for boys,
Likewise props for proes;
The salvation army comes to me
For all their holy clothes.
My stock of boots cannot be beat,
For ladies and for men;
Every sole is warranted
To stick to the upper-ten.

Chorus–

So if you want a suit of clothes, &c.

A tribute to one Penny Street outfitters', sung by local comic Peter Pollock at the
Bird-in-Hand Hotel in Darwen Street.

141 Wood J., clothes dlr
143 Rigby Mrs. E., fried
    fish dealer
Audley range
132 & 134 Hindle T., grcr
118 Murphy Mrs. Mary
108 Pickering T., weaver
98 Gill R., tea mixer
96 Haworth Mrs. Betty
94 Shorrock J., spinner
Scotland road
90 Ashworth Mrs. Alice
90 Ashworth J. (Exors.of),
    coal merchants
88 Fairhurst J. & Son,
    joiners
86 Bray Mr. Benjamin
86 Duckworth T. E., coal
    dealer
80 Dean Miss E.
66 Grice F., clothes dlr
38 Hargreaves D., spinner
36 Caton A., grinder
30 Marsden R., overlookr
10 Hartley R., bootmaker

CHORLTON ST.

2 Chadwick Mr. Wm.
4 Heald T., mechanic
6 Stopforth W., cloggr(j.)
8 Bentley D., overlooker
10 Royston Misses
12 Parkinson Mrs. Margt.
14 Parker M., joiner (j.)
16 Mounsey J., shuttle
    maker (j.)
18 Guest R., smith (j.)
20 Hutchinson E. D.,
    printer (j.)
24 Hodgkinson G., shuttle
    maker (j.)
26 Morphew W. J., dis-
    penser
28 Chadwick J. B., pavior
30 Greenwood Mrs. Ann
32 Chadwick J., pavior
34 Yates O., overlooker

CHURCH STREET.

3 Austin C. R., watchmkr
5 & 7 Walmsley W.,
    dining-rooms
9 & 11 *Union Club*; W.
    Thompson, hon. sec.
13 Levers W. H., clothier
King William street
17 Sagar R. H. & J.,
    jewellers
19 Scott G., hatter
21 Walsh T., clothier
Conservative Club; T.
    Preston, secretary

Thwaites Arcade
Lancashire & York-
    shire Bank ; A. Sug-
    den, manager
Shorrock fold
    Lord H., *Star Inn*
    Walmsley J., care-
    taker
    Marsden M., paper
    bag maker
    Patent Metallic
    Fibre, &c., Co.
31 Cheshire J., woollen
    merchant
33 & 35 Crossley R.,
    general dealer
37 & 39 Pickering P.,
    brush manufacturer
41 *Express and Standard*
    Offices
Victoria street
49 Parker M., bootmaker
51 Forbes A., *Golden Lion*
53 Maypole Dairy Co.
55 Cowburn T. L.,
    umbrella manufactr
57 Astley A., stationer
59 Robinson E., fruiterer
61 Wilson R., dining-rms
63 Appleby J. & Sons,
    millers
63 Leach E. C., agent
65 Pollard Dr. W. R.
62 Cronkshaw E., *White
    Bull Hotel*
60 Butterworth Mrs. E.
    A., confectioner
58 Myers J., brush mnfr
56 London & Midland
    Bank, Ltd.; J. W.
    Pearson, manager
56 Shackleton R. & Son,
    millers
54 Salisbury W. & Hamer,
    auctioneers
52 Ollerenshaw G. & Co.,
    tea dealers
50 Riding R., bootmaker
48 Dunkerley W., boot-
    maker
Temple court
46 Baldwin J. (Exors. of),
    ironmongers
42 & 44 Metcalfe's mantle
    warehouse
40 Booth E. H. & Co.,
    Ltd., tea dealers
40a Pickup J. & Co., spirit
    merchants
Conservative Club
    (Junior) ; C. H.
    Whewell, secretary
38 Bonney J., india rubber
    dealer

36 Bramwell & Co., hair-
    dressers
34 Briggs T. E., draper
32 Lawson S., tea dealer
30 Johnson T., printer
28 Stirrup T., bootmaker
26 Wright G. & Sons,
    dyers
22 & 24 Addison & Co.,,
    spirit merchants
20 Wigan Coal & Iron
    Co., Ltd.; R. Spencer,
    agent
Parish Church
18 Lamm A. B., *Old Bull
    Hotel*
    Cunliffes, Brooks, &
    Co. (Old Bank)
8, 10, & 12 Dewhurst's
    clothiers
6 Wilson W., hosier
4 Sames W., spirit mrcht
2 Aspden Miss A., millnr

CICELY STREET.

Baynes John, Cicely
    Bridge mill
Hartley Bros., Alma
    mill
Wigan Coal and Iron
    Co., Ltd.
Cicely lane
Blackburn J., pntsmn
Salisbury E., cashier
Hart street
10 Eastwood J., shopkpr
8 Sharples J. M., loomer
6 Hartley Mr. William
4 Robinson W., painter
2 Atherton F., tripe dlr

CLARENCE ST.

Till Mr. Jph., Clarence
    villa
Nash Rev. F. P., M.A.,
    St. John's vicarage

CLARENDON RD.

10 Chadwick G., contrctr
12 Wilding S., clogger (j.)
14 Calderbank Mr. John
16 Barton J., greengrocer
18 Crossley Mr. Henry

CLAYTON STREET.

1 *Weavers' Association*;
    J. Cross, secretary
1 *Cardroom, &c., Asso-
    ciation*; P. Maguire,
    secretary

JOHN BALDWIN,

CHURCH-ST., BLACKBURN,

IRON AND STEEL MERCHANT,

MILL, MACHINE, AND GENERAL FURNISHING

IRONMONGER,

MANUFACTURER OF

KITCHEN RANGES, SMOKE JACKS, &c.,

HOT WATER APPARATUS

For Churches, Green Houses, &c., fitted on the most scientific principles.

HURDLES, GATES,

SCOTCH FENCING, PALLISADES,

Scale Beams, Iron Bedsteads, &c.

A large and choice assortment of REGISTER GRATES, FENDERS, FIRE IRONS, &c.

WHITESMITH AND BELLHANGER.

Baldwin's, shown here in a trade directory of 1870-71, stood on the corner of *Church Street* and *Temple Court*.

92, DARWEN STREET,

BLACKBURN *Nov 14* 190 8

M *Bolton Mrs*

Bought of E. FINDLAY,

WHOLESALE PORK BUTCHER.

Maker of the "Perfection" Pork Pies   Ham and Bacon Curer.   Lard Refiner

Pork Sausage and Bacon Factor.   The Trade supplied on reasonable terms

2 | 1 2

10 4

92, DARWEN STREET,

BLACKBURN *June 3* 1907

M r *Bolton*   *Bolton Rd*

Bought of HOLDEN BROS.

(LATE FINDLAY,)

WHOLESALE & RETAIL PORK BUTCHERS.

Makers of the "Perfection" Pork Pies   Ham and Bacon Curers.   Lard Refiners.
Genuine Pork Sausage and Bacon Factors.   The Trade supplied on reasonable terms

1907

May 31 To 3 lb Pork   2 | 1 2

When 92, *Darwen Street* changed hands, so did the stationery, along with the stout butcher's pig!

DARWEN STREET

BOLTON ROAD

Darwen Street leads from the remains of a medieval church to the site of Blackburn's old town moor between Nova Scotia and Grimshaw Park, but today it looks like little more than an isolated side street. Before the industrial revolution, the path of the Blakewater under Darwen Street marked the town boundary, and ten acres between what are now Park Road and Great Bolton Street were set aside as common ground to be used for the sustenance of the poor, or for recreation, or military training (a gunpowder magazine was kept at the junction of the two roads until the mid-Nineteenth century). Even in Victorian times, before King William Street came into its own, the pavements between that junction and the old market cross were crammed with stalls and penny bazaars run by, amongst others, *'Marks & Spencer's'*, and resounding to the bustle of housewives examining the goods on show.

Darwen Street had been a trading site as long as there had been a market at its end in front of the churchyard. Indeed, it has been rightly said that, by the 1820s, it was the location of the principal tradesmen's premises in the town – over a hundred of them, in fact. As the number of mills in the industrial districts of Blackburn expanded, hamlets like Nova Scotia and Islington were drawn into the body of the town, and Darwen Street carried their goods and workers. Furthermore, buildings like the Dandy Mill owned by *Bannister Eccles and Co.*, as well as several dozen accompanying workers' cottages, were springing up in Darwen Street itself. The neighbouring areas of Mincing Lane (formerly Back Lane) and Market Street Lane prospered, and Great Bolton Street and Bolton Road were crammed with pubs, shops and workshops serving the mills to the South of the town and – most lucrative of all – their hard-pressed workforce. All along the now deserted streets between Darwen Street Bridge and the Royal Infirmary, craftsmen laboured in basements or outhouses of mills, or in neighbouring warehouses and workshops, or along the canalside, making rope or brushes, or decorating, plumbing or in joinery. At the end of a hard day's work, they might in the 1890s have visited any of nearly two dozen licensed premises on the short (but not necessarily brief!) two-thirds-of-a-mile jaunt from Infirmary Road to Darwen Street. In a one-sided street of less than 500 yards, Great Bolton Street alone boasted eight pubs – or one every fifth door! Further out of town, where it diverged from the railway, Bolton Road had a wider variety of shops including chemists, grocers and shoe-shine merchants, as well as many private homes, most of which have now disappeared – although the small number of

J Neville's general store in *Darwen Street* stood for nearly a century. Started in the 1870s selling hardware from Bolton Road as well, Neville's grew to include nos. 94-98 at the bottom of Mincing Lane. The shop offered a range of goods, and is remembered by Blackburn shoppers for childhood indulgences such as visits to see Santa Claus. In 1906, when the stationery on the left was in use, Neville's shop kept him in comfort at Raven's Wing Villa on Revidge, and, although now demolished, traded until the 1960s.

ESTABLISHED 1854.

JOHN HAYES,

Rope, Twine, Cotton Banding,

and Driving Rope Manufacturer,

61, DARWEN STREET,

BLACKBURN.

WORKS:—LOWER HOLLIN BANK STREET.

DARWEN STREET,

Telephone 118y.

Blackburn,_____190__

Specialities:

Waltham Watches.

Glass Shades and Stands.

Wreathes and Covers.

Publicans' Sundries

Gold and Silver Jewellery.

Cutlery, Toys, &c.

Bought of J. NEVILLE,

WHOLESALE GENERAL MERCHANT.

Telephone 74 Y.

Oh, Mother! Mother!
don't forget the

NOK-O
DRY SOAP.

It's Washing Day
To-morrow.
ASK YOUR GROCER FOR IT.

Terms—Eggs, Net Cash in 7 days.

10, HIGHFIELD ROAD,

Blackburn,_____190__

Bought of W. H. Pickop,

EGG & PROVISION MERCHANT.

GOLD MEDAL AWARDED.
BLACKBURN, 1890.

HOME-CURED AND HOME-COOKED TONGUES A SPECIALITY.

Lang's Map of 1739 shows that **Darwen Street**, the route to the church and market, was the most densely populated part of the town before the Industrial Revolution. As the papers here show, it was still busy at the start of the 20th century.

remaining properties includes some of the oldest shops and wholesalers in Blackburn, dating back to the Eighteenth century.

By the end of the Nineteenth century, Darwen Street was notable as a principal artery of the tram system, and for some of the largest shops in Blackburn, often on several floors, matched by roomy nearby pubs, halls and hotels offering extensive music-hall style entertainment. The older, squat cottages and shops which survived were overshadowed or replaced by institutions such as the Higher Grade School (since become the Diocesan offices) in the churchyard, or the impressive Central Post Office, opened in 1907.

It was not until some time after the Second World War that Darwen Street began to be drained of its life. Whilst other parts of the town were undoubtedly developing, the old road to market still had over 90 businesses in 1966, and centuries-old pubs like the *'Legs O'Man'* still served customers until the 1970s. However, a location like Darwen Street was bound to suffer from the redevelopments of the '60s and '70s, and the sound of builders' plant digging the foundations of *'Debenhams'* in 1977 must have struck a funereal note with the shopkeepers still in Darwen Street. Now it is without its factories, Post Office, (recently reopened as a pub, *'The Postal Order'*) or indeed many of its shops, and cut off from major precincts and transport links, the street's businesses have struggled to survive. Nonetheless, Darwen Street is one of the few thoroughfares the length of whose path the visitor can still look, as uninterrupted as at the turn of the century or earlier – however much the buildings at the roadside might have changed.

Above: Most provisions and perishable goods were brought from outside the area. All forms of transport were used, even the canal, as this cargo declaration illustrates. Cargoes carried by canal were stored in the Eanam or Bolton Road warehouses.

Right: Grocer and chemist James Bolton is a good example of the small-scale shopkeepers who served the growing suburbs of Blackburn at the turn of the century, buying goods around town, especially from wholesale warehouses in the centre. He lived nearby in Highfield Road and then Infirmary Road. His shop at 159 Bolton Road still stands - one of the few Victorian buildings left on a once-busy thoroughfare of homes, mills and two dozen pubs.

159, BOLTON ROAD,

Blackburn, _____ 18

M

JAMES BOLTON,
WHOLESALE & RETAIL GROCER & PROVISION DEALER.

Bolton's
Danish
Kiel is
Delicious.

Bolton's
Tea at 1/4
Best in
Town.

Bolton's
Tea at 1/6
is a
Perfect
Luxury.

Bolton's
Tea at 2/-
is the talk
of the
Town.

Bolton's
Butter
is equal to
New.

Bolton's
Eggs
are Fresh
three
times a
week.

Bolton's
for
Beautiful
Mild
Cheese.

We sell *Crawford's*

CREAM CRACKERS
ROYAL GINGER (NEW)
MAYFAIR
OVAL RICH TEA
MEXICAN (GINGER FLAVOUR)
KIEL FINGERS &C

190

Bot. of

BOLTON'S
CHEAP GROCERY AND PROVISION STORES,
159, Bolton Road, Novas, BLACKBURN.

159, BOLTON ROAD, NOVAS,

Blackburn, ...*March 11*..19 1 0

M..

Bought of **BOLTON'S**
Cheap Grocery and Provision Stores.

One Packet of
"LIVELY POLLY"
DRY SOAP
goes further than three of
any other.

41

96 Eccles J. M., turnr (j.)
94 Richardson S., fitter
92 Swarbrick C., weaver
90 Standing J., grocer
 Polly street
86 Monk J., fruiterer
84 Haworth Mrs. J.,
 shopkeeper
54 Marsh J. H., grocer
 Cecil street
52 Morris Mrs. M., shpkpr
 Hollinshead Mill Co.,
 Limited
34 Clegg D., overlooker
30 Cook R., confectioner
 Dugdale John & Sons,
 Daisyfield mill
10 Briscoe G., moulder

DALTON STREET.

2 Middleton Samuel
4 Jackson Mrs. Dorothy
6 Jackson W., fruiterer
14 Whalley W., spinner
20 Briggs Mr. George

DARWEN STREET.

1, 3, & 5 Munro G. & Co.,
 spirit merchants
 Higher Grade School;
 H. Boddy
7 Booth & Co., chemists
9 & 11 Taylor R., *County Arms*
13 Sagar J., watchmaker
15 Millward & Fairbrother
 confectioners
17 Brownlee R., *Queen's Head*
 Dandy walk
 Stott Wm., Limtd,
 smiths
 Blackburn and District Bill Posting
 Co., Limited; W.
 Rollinson, sec.
19 Baines T., fishmonger
21 Polding J. F., corn
 merchant
23 Fish Mrs E., stationer
25 Schofield J., confectnr
27 Hargreaves E., tripe dlr
29 Eastham Miss S.,
 florist
31 Ingram & Co., bedding
 manufacterers
 Venetian hall
 Seed E., venetian
 blind maker
 Gregson T. & Son
 wood carvers
35 Wallace J., bootmaker

37 Bailey J., ironmonger
39 Heys J. (Exors. of),
 painters
41 Prize Dairy Butter Co.
43 & 45 Thompson J.,
 Merchants' Hotel
 Jubilee street
47 Blackburn Finance &
 Loan Co.
47 Blackburn Clothing
 Club
47 & 49 Cheetham C.,
 plumber
51 Sager W., tailor
53 Smith E., piano dealer
55 Brierley S., smllware
 dealer
57 Sumner J. W., draper
59 Hayes J., ropemaker
61 King W., draper
63 Bolton W., photogrphr
65 Fenton W. J., carver
67 Davis F., agent
69 Pye R., mill furnisher
71 Peel J., butcher
73 & 75 Alston T., *Stokers' Arms*
77 Fulton R., fruiterer
 George street
79 Walsh Miss S., mlnr
81 Hindle & Yates, mlnrs
 Stones W. & Sons,
 timber merchants
 Slater A., hairdresser
111 Spence F., confectnr
113 Dowhurst A., eating ho
115 Greenhalgh W., hairdresser
115a Ashton E., tobacconist
117 Baines Mrs. A. A.,
 tripe dealer
119 Eccles T., fruiterer
121 Cunliffe C., tinner
 Park road and Great Bolton street
 Canterbury street
136 Cooper E., *Duke of York*
134 Carr H., baker
132 Grimshaw W. H.,
 chemist
130 Butcher C., bootmkr
124 Brown Bros., bakers
122 Birkett J., china dealer
110 Ibbotson T. E., draper
118 Seed Cycle Co., cycle
 manufacturers
 Baron's yard
 Driver A., reed manufr
 Brooks G. W., builder
100 Universal Furnishing
 Company
98 Palatine Art Co., picture dealers

94 Neville J., general dlr
92 Findlay Mrs. E., pork
 butcher
90 Orrell T., saddler
88 Riding D., bootmaker
86 Hargreaves E., tripe
 dealer
84 Munroe Mrs. A., confr
82 Dixon Mrs. S., *George Hotel*
 Dixon & Slater, cab
 proprietors
 Weir street
78 & 80 Prest T., grocer
76aCatterall R. H., registrar of births
76 Gregson D., baby linen
 dealer
74 Wilson A. D., dyer
72 Knowles C., printer
70 Cross R., cabinet mkr
68 Howson R., ironmngr
66 Talbot I., fruiterer
64 Mellor J., hairdresser
62 Mercer J., stationer
60 Smith F., watchmaker
58 Gudgeon T., butcher
56 Holme Mrs. M., eating
 house
54 Isherwood W. & J.,
 painters
 Mill lane
48, 50, and 52 Harrison
 R. W. & Co., rubber
 merchants
46 Mercer E., bootmaker
44 Sellers Miss E. A,
 confectioner
42 and 40 Sharples J. B.,
 draper
38 Sharples T., hatter
36 Eglen A. E., herbalist
34 Greenwood J. & Sons,
 corn millers
 St. Peter street
32 Yates D., chemist
28 and 30 Barnes J. & Co.,
 drapers
26 Kisielowski C., grocer
24 Bean C. B., saddler
22 Counsell G., draper
18 Tattersall T., *Eagle and Child Hotel*
16 Constantine T. & Son,
 butchers
 Market Street lane
12 Welding A., saddler
10 Thomas J. G., tobcnst
8a Whittaker Jas., draper
8 Hamer R. & Sons,
 ironmongers
 Fleming square
 Cunliffes, Brooks & Co.,
 bankers

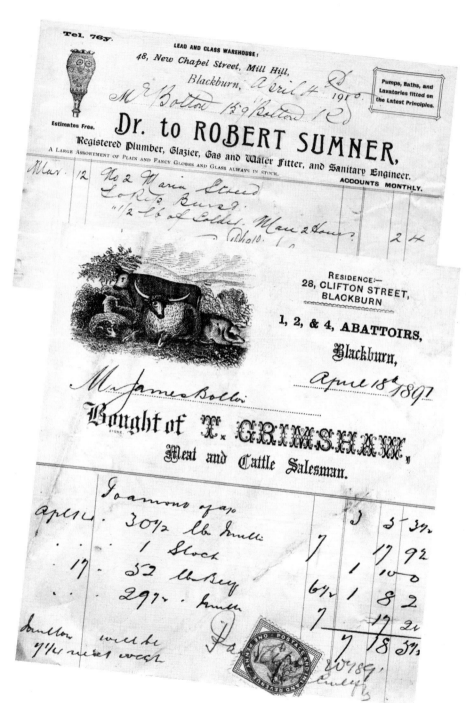

The stamp affixed to a receipt, as above, showed the due tax had been paid.

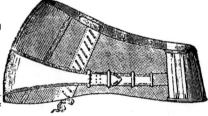
Farnworth's was one of the high class shops to be found in *King William Street*. This advert from a local directory shows some of their wares, from the days when only the wealthy could afford to be ill.

KING WILLIAM STREET

King William Street is a relative newcomer amongst Blackburn's town centre shopping places. It was first created in 1832, two years into the reign of William IV, by the demolition of five centuries-old shops and a warehouse between Church Street and Livesey Croft, which stood at the junction of Lord Street and Livesey Street, roughly where King William Street comes to an end today. Livesey Street ran from this point to Thunder Alley, (as Town Hall Street was originally known) and retained its name until the 1850s, whilst King William Street was no more than a conduit between it and the Old Market Place.

The former was swallowed up by the latter as, during the second half of the Nineteenth Century, Blackburn's newest and most prestigious buildings sprang up alongside its route. 1848 saw the completion of two years' work by the town's Improvement Commissioners with the opening of the new Market House on 1,693 square yards of land formerly known as *'Sudell's Croft'*, and now covered by the shopping precinct on the East side of King William Street. Costing £10,000, this was Blackburn's first great public building, described as *"unequalled by any market house in Lancashire"*, and the open space to its side and rear became the venue of mass public meetings and the Easter Fair. The hall's tolls were initially collected by John Pickup, a draper whose shop was at 3, King William Street. The Town Hall, incorporating the police offices and courts, was built alongside, on the site of a bowling green, in similar Italianate grandeur by 1856, and the Cotton Exchange across the street was opened in 1865. Sudell Cross acquired a handsome public gas lamp presented by Mayor John Smith in 1868, although sadly he was eventually unable to pay for it, and it caused a fatal accident fourteen years later. In 1872, a fish market was added to the Market Hall, and the Museum and Library just off King William street opened in 1874. Since the 1850s , shops had been springing up from Albert Buildings on the corner with Town Hall Street to Sudell Cross and into Preston New Road, where the imposing frontage of Aspden Buildings appeared in 1886.

King William Street at the turn of the century was Blackburn's shopping showpiece: as well as these noble and impressive buildings, it had prestigious hotels like the *'St. Leger'* and the *'Prince of Wales'*, and both the *'Conservative'* and *'Cobden Reform Clubs'*. Around grand shop buildings named after Albert, Victoria or Peel, or with proud titles like *Kensington Place*, there were 300 stalls outside the Market Hall twice weekly, and by 1900 some seventy-three permanent shops – many

2-44 King William Street, inclusive of the shops below, ran from where Debenhams now stands to Victoria Buildings, (at the top of King William Mall). It was Blackburn's 'Hyde Park Corner', graced by E.H.Booth's cafe.

10, King William Street,
Blackburn, June 30th 1906

NAT. TEL. 536

Mr Jas Bolton Grocer Nova Scotia

TO C. A. CRITCHLEY & CO., DR.

Pharmaceutical Chemists, .
. . Wholesale Druggists.

Drysalters, Spice, Seed & Oil Merchants; Paint and Colourmen.

May 16 1 gl Bragg
June 16 1 x gl
18 To pro

TELEPHONE 331.

TELEGRAPHIC ADDRESS "TATTERSALL" BLACKBURN.

32 & 34 King William St. BLACKBURN. Oct 3 1893

Mr James Bolton

Bot of William Tattersall

Cheese Factor, Ham and Bacon Curer.

→ IMPORTER OF IRISH & AMERICAN PROVISIONS. —

TERMS CASH.

SPECIAL SELECTIONS IN KIEL BUTTER.

36. King William St

TELEPHONE No 23.

Blackburn Nov 1 1893

Mr J Bolton

Bot of James Hargreaves,

WHOLESALE TOBACCONIST & CIGAR MERCHANT.

Tattersall and **Hargreaves**, above, were typical of the leading figures who were neighbours in *King William Street*. William Tattersall was twice Mayor of Blackburn, and James Hargreaves founded the Girls' High School at Spring Mount. The former was a strict teetotaller and non-smoker, and the latter a keen huntsman and socialiser as well as a tobacconist, and many (but amicable) were the debates they had as they travelled to work together along Preston New Road in the 1900s.

ONLY Address, 36, KING WILLIAM STREET. BLACKBURN.

W. Farnworth moved to No. 49 in 1855, and was still there in the 1890s. Supplier of table water for Royal visits to Blackburn, he boasted *"Nothing of an inferior nature is permitted on the premises"*!

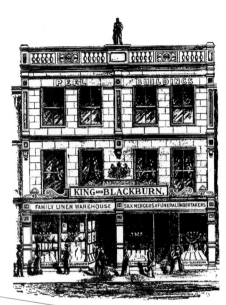

County Tailoring, for all their world renown, showed that the printed spelling error is nothing new!

39 - 57 King William Street were the numbers facing the Market Hall — now the modern precinct — built during the 1850s in a style reflecting Blackburn's growing stature at the time, and dealing in more luxurious goods than had previously been common in the town. **Peel Buildings**, Nos. 45 & 47, above, was built in 1854, and later housed Furness' drapers.

packed into different storeys of the same prime site – including seven tailors and drapers, six milliners, five hosiers and glovers, and various dyers, dealers in silk, wool or baby linen, athletic outfitters, jewellers, hairdressers, and boot, shoe and umbrella shops. Many will still remember the days when the names *'Furness'*, *'Burton'* and *'Dowson'* marked out King William Street as the place to go if you wanted to dress to impress!

Much of this evidence of Blackburn's glory remains today. However, King William Street is also the scene of some of the most controversial changes in the redevelopments of the Twentieth Century. The Cotton Exchange – never completed – became a cinema in 1924, and in 1934 Peel Buildings and the statue of the former Prime Minister atop it were demolished to make way for *'Marks & Spencer's'*. The most sweeping changes came after 1964, when the beloved town clock was pulled down in front of a crowd of hundreds, many tearful at the loss of the landmark, shortly to be followed by the Market Hall and nearby buildings. By 1971 the second phase of the redevelopment of the town centre had obliterated any real sign of Victoria Street, Lord Street and Cort Street, which had been such central features of the town plan during Blackburn's years of expansion. Six years later, Phase Three was begun, severing King William Street and blocking the view from Church Street by putting *'Debenhams'* in the plot occupied a century and a half earlier by the shops destroyed to create King William Street. Ironically, the newest and most substantial development of shops had in this respect restored the street plan of Georgian times.

50 *Head Quarters 3rd L.A.V.*; Capt. F. A. Tighe, adjutant
48 Jepson W., draper
France street.
46 Aspden M., yeast mcht
44 Southworth E., tobcnst
42 Hamilton G., fruiterer
40 Aspden G., printer
36 & 38 Painter F., *Royal Hotel*
Paradise lane.
26 to 34 Bottomley R. M., clothier
Paradise terrace.
1 Millan Mrs. E., aprnts
3 Read Bros., drysalters
5 Clarkson Mr. O.
Friends' Meeting House
Old Barracks.
Blackburn Bass & Fibre Co.
22 Turner J., furn remvr
18a, 20, & 22 Barrington J., furn manufactr
18 Hayhurst H., agent
16 Needham T., chiropdst
14 Haworth W., watchmaker
12 Walsh R. & Co., herbalists
10 Byrne Miss H., confr
6 & 8 Crossley T., *Angel Inn*
4 *Overseers' Office*; J. B. Margerison, assist overseer
4 *Superintendent Registrar's Office*; Henry Whittaker
2 Robinson & Sons, solicitors
2 *Coroner's Office*; H. J. Robinson

KING WILLIAM STREET.

1 & 3 Eccleston James, *Prince of Wales Hotel*
5 Jones J., draper
7 Melia D. & Co., Ltd., grocers
9 Brooke C., ironmonger
11 Robinson H. & Sons, grocers
13 Holden Mrs. E., mllnr
15 Sellers T., butcher
17 London Rubber Co.
Lord street
19 Whittaker Wm., *St. Leger Hotel*

21 Pegram J. & Co., tea dealers
25 Lipton T. J., provision merchant
27 Webster & Co., tea dealers
29 Mercer N., grocer
31 Denham R. & Co., booksellers
33 Dickson & Nuttall, drapers
Manchester & County Bank, Ltd.; J. S. Pollitt, manager
New Market street
39 & 41 Stonehouse F., draper
Peel buildings
43 Pinder W., china dlr
45 & 47 King & Blackburn, drapers
49 Farnworth W. & Son, chemists
51 Sefton J., grocer
53 Cash & Co., hatters
55 Welch J., jeweller
57 Gibson J. & H., tea dealers
Town Hall street
59 & 61 Downs H. H., *Exchange Hotel*
Exchange flags
Brothers M., solicitor
Cowburn F., umbrella manufacturer
Blackburn Exchange Co., Ltd.; L. Edleston, secretary
Exchange buildings
Holt J. T., brewery agent
Barton J. S., junr., hardware merchant
Slater & Co., mineral water manufactrs
Cobden Reform Club; J. E. Hand, sec.
Whitehead E., butchr
Geddes & Marsh, Berlin wool dealers
Baines & Allen, hosrs
Cook J. W., *Grapes Inn*
Sudell cross
84 & 82 Sutton H. P., mantle warehouse
80 Garland A. P., chemist
78aBurrows Mrs. W., baby linen dealer
78 Metcalfe J. R., bookseller
76 Abbott O., draper
74 Bennett Mrs. E. E., Berlin wool dealer
72 Coupe M., draper

70 Troop Miss E., confctr
68aJohnson Bros., dyers
68 Gelson L. A., hairdrsr
66 Turner W. E., baker
64 Smalley H., ironmonger
62 Whitehead F. N., chemist
60 Kay A. & Bro., jewllrs
58 Stow W., draper
Library street
Manchester & Liverpool District Bank, Ltd.; R. A. Pippet, manager
Exchange street
Town Hall
Town Clerk's Office; R. E. Fox
Borough Treasurer's Office; J. H. Bailey
Borough Magistrates' Clerk's Office; M. Brothers
Market Hall
44 Goodson R., Limited, mantle warehouse
42 Bennett & Co., hatters
40 Parker T., boot manufacturer
38 Vickers & Co., clothiers
36 Hargreaves J., tobacco merchant
32 & 34 Tattersall W., provision merchant
30 Constantine R. H., general dealer
28 Mellor Bros., hosiers and glovers
26 Manufacturing Alliance Co., clothrs
Lord street
24 Boothman J., butcher
22 Maypole Dairy Co.
20 Webster T., hosier and glover
18 Metcalfe W. A., jewllr
12, 14, & 16 Worswick Bros., drapers and furriers
10 Critchley T., chemist
8 Charnley J., bootmkr
6 Stead & Simpson, Ltd., boot manufacturers
Old Cross Chambers
Crook T. C. M., archt
Stones G. W., solicitor
Blackburn Advertiser Office; F. Stones, proprietor
4aMason H., oyster dlr
4 Walsh Miss Henrietta, milliner
2 Garstang J., tobaccnst

49

22, NEW MARKET STREET, *Blackburn,* Sep 2 189 2

M J Bolton

Bought of BANNISTER BROS.,

Wholesale Grocers and Tea Merchants.

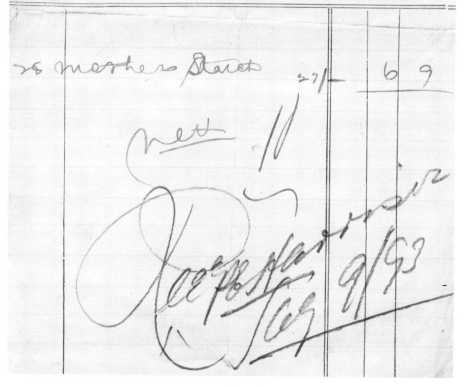

THE SYDNEY COMPANY'S
LIEBIG'S EXTRACT.

FOR SOUPS, SAUCES, GRAVIES, INVALIDS.

ARTHUR H, HASSALL, M.D., SAYS: "IT WILL STAND SECOND TO NONE IN QUALITY AND PURITY.'

THE SYDNEY is supplied to THE ADMIRALTY, and used in H M. SHIPS and NAVAL HOSPITALS.

28 Mothers Starch   27/-   6   9

nett

RICHMOND TERRACE

The consumers of Victorian and Edwardian Blackburn, like those of today, did not only spend their income on goods, but also on services; and as today, certain of those professional and practical services were provided from offices gathered in a particular part of the town. Richmond Terrace and its environs are such an area.

Like King William Street, Richmond Terrace had no properties on it until the early 1820s, and was even known by another name – *'West Street'*. This path meeting Northgate just below Limbrick led to Richmond Hill, the area in front of St. John's Church. It acquired its more upmarket name as, during the 1820s and '30s, the impressive row of characteristically Georgian houses still standing on its North side was constructed. In the 1850s these were the homes of millowners, doctors, teachers and some better-off grocers whose business premises were elsewhere in town, and in many senses, therefore, these were the seats of influence and decision-making in Blackburn. As the second half of the century wore on, these properties were increasingly used as offices rather than homes by the professional classes. At the same time, halls and offices of an obviously commercial or public nature sprang up on the open ground facing the houses on the South side of the Terrace. By the early years of this century, Richmond Terrace was the address of a string of architects, assurance brokers, surveyors, estate agents, accountants and solicitors. Here in the 1900s were to be found the headquarters of Witton Estates, the Chamber of Commerce, the local Charities' Organisation, the Chancery and Income Tax Offices, the factory inspector's and Infirmary offices, and the County and district Liberal Party's headquarters. Still visible today on the South side of the Terrrace are the Masonic Hall, Richmond Chambers where the Blackburn Law Association, founded in 1883, held its meetings in the law library, and – for relaxation – the Turkish Baths. When the Great War brought rationing, it was in Richmond Terrace that the Food Committee set up its offices in 1917.

At the other end of Library (now Museum) Street, an increasing number of services were at the turn of the century being provided by the Borough Council. Gas supplies has become municipally owned in 1878; the council took control of electricity and public transport in 1894 and 1898 respectively. This was also the time when the Corporation undertook a concerted campaign to improve public sanitation and regulate trade by shopkeepers who had previously been able to sell short measures or adulterate foods. A string of Acts of Parliament passed between the late 1870s and the early Twentieth Century forbade shopkeepers to give false

Richmond Terrace looks today much as it has since the time Queen Victoria came to the throne. It has been the hub of Blackburn's legal and property services for the last century, as the papers on the left illustrate, a role confirmed by the arrival from Ainsworth Street of more solicitors' firms with the post-war redevelopment of the town.

26, Richmond Terrace,

Blackburn.

27/10 1926

R. DUCKWORTH,
COLLECTOR OF TAXES.
HOUSE & ESTATE AGENT.

34, Richmond Terrace,

Blackburn, April 1891

Dear Sir,

Yourself to

I beg to remind you that your

half-year's Ground Rent will becom

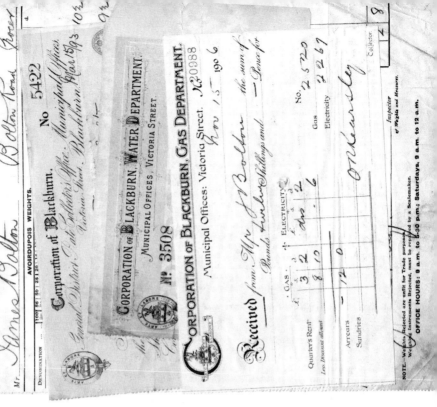

BLACKBURN.

THE TOWN HALL.

The *Town Hall* took pride of place in the directory of the 1880s from whose first page this picture comes. During the late nineteenth century, the Corporation took on the responsibility for many new services, for which the citizens had to pay. Still, with quarterly charges for gas, electricity and water adding up to the equivalent of just over 76p, Mr. Bolton's bills look very reasonable today.

descriptions of their wares, or to swindle customers by practices such as adding sand to brown sugar, glass to salt, or water to beer or butter. Whilst shopkeepers usually welcomed the elimination of cowboy competitors this meant, they had to put up with the interference of the town hall bureaucrat – and the added expense passed on in the rates. Blackburn's Grocers' Association took a particular pride in rooting out *'faked goods'*, and worked closely with the council. Mayor Alderman Crossley commended the trade in 1912 as *"receivers and purveyors of news on all subjects"*, and the following year the Corporation's Health Committee found no adulteration in 177 samples of goods stocked by the Association's members. There were some prosecutions, but often of shops run by outsiders – *'Casey and Co.'*, an Irish firm in Park Road, which also had branches in Bolton, Liverpool and Manchester, was found by inspectors in 1900 to be selling *'butter'* over four-fifths of which consisted of other fats or water!

Although surrounded by much newer roads, and in the shadow of larger modern buildings, the streets around St. John's Church and Sudell Cross – including Museum Street, and parts of Limbrick, Victoria Street and James Street – probably retain as much of their turn-of-the-century character as any in Blackburn. Some courts and corners of houses and offices to the side of Richmond Terrace have been pulled down, but that elegant row of Georgian town houses would still be fit to grace any screen adaptation of Jane Austen's or George Eliot's works today.

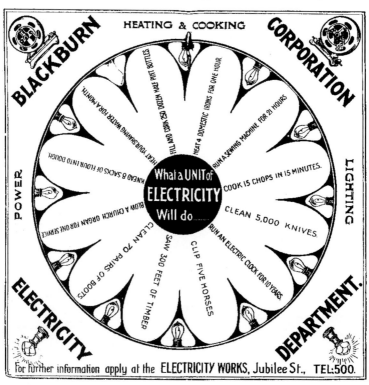

THE PHARMACY,
NOVA SCOTIA,
Blackburn, *Nova*
May 15 1906

Mr. *Bolton*
Dr. to

Wm. Butterfield, M.Ph.Sc.
WHOLESALE CHEMIST, DRUGGIST, & DRYSALTER.

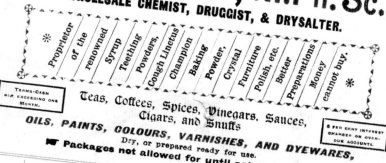

Proprietor of the renowned Syrup Teething Powders, Cough Linctus Champion Baking Powder, Crystal Furniture Polish, etc. Better Preparations Money cannot buy.

TERMS-CASH
NOT EXCEEDING ONE
MONTH.

Teas, Coffees, Spices, Vinegars, Sauces,
Cigars, and Snuffs

5 PER CENT INTEREST
CHARGED ON OVER-
DUE ACCOUNTS.

OILS, PAINTS, COLOURS, VARNISHES, AND DYEWARES,
Dry, or prepared ready for use.
☞ Packages not allowed for until actually received.

1 dz 6ª Cough Bottles 4/3.   4/3

RESIDENCE
1, WELLINGTON ST
(ST JOHN'S)
Telephone 130X.

—❈ Market Place, ❈—
BLACKBURN, *Jan 22* 190

Mr James Bolton

BOUGHT OF A. BOLTON,
FRUIT & POTATO MERCHANT, CARROTS, &c.

Terms Cash on delivery.
DIXBURY & SONS, LTD.

Empties to be returned in 14 days.
EMPTIES.   PRICE.   £   s.   d.

Jan 13 10 cwt carrots   1 - 0 - 0

RICHMOND HILL.

7 Bolton Mrs. M. J., Hindle Arms
9 Cookson L. A., earthenware dealer
11 Fletcher M. A., earthenware dealer
13 Holden J. T., messngr Townson W., cabt mkr Cross E. & Sons, painters
Cooper E. J., cabt mkr
Lenz W., builder
Lomax B., boot maker Tontine street
Burniston C. H,, coopr
Shorrock J., joiner Kirkham lane
Isherwood Mrs. E., cabinet maker
Mellor R. & Co., cart cover makers

RICHMOND TER.

1 Bullough E. J., accnt
1 Crossley S., solicitor
2 Surveyor of Taxes Office; T. Blackwell
2 Income Tax Office; D. B. Woolfall, clerk
3 Lord S., dentist
4 N. and N. E. L. Cotton Spinners' and Manufacturers' Association; R. Taylor, sec
5 Hayward T. S., music professor
6 Chamber of Commerce
6 Eccles J. & S., yarn agents
6 Watson J., agent
6 Watson W., agent
7 Pickop Mr. John, J.P.
8 Wilding & Son, solctrs
9 Parkinson F. J., archt
9 Roberts & Verne, law stationers
9 Charity Organization; M. Brothers, sec
9 StarrBowkett Building Society; J. & F. Imison, secretaries
10 Stones & Gradwell, architects
10 Brierley & Holt, archts
10 Brierley & Howard, patent agents
11 Ratcliffe & Kenyon, share brokers
11 Witton Estate Office, R. J. Howard
12 Watson J. S., M.A., M.D
13 Higson H,, surveyor

13 Farnworth R. D., flour merchant
14 Hargreaves John, solr
14 Stirrup W., architect
15 Sandbach J. C. H., architect
15 Haworth J., accountnt
15 Infirmary Office; N. A. Smith, sec
15 St. John's Ambulance Association; N. A. Smith & J. Haworth, hon. secs
16 Morley E.S., M.D., J.P.
17 Leeming A., L.D.S., dentist
18 Needham R. C., solr.
18 Lonsdale W. & Son, share brokers
19 Y.W.C. Association; Miss Eddleston, supt
20 Burrows W. B., dentist
21 Rushton (E.) Son & Kenyon, auctioneers
21 Scott E. J., agent
21 Preston D. J., solicitor
22 Barnish R. D., solicitor
22 Wilkinson W. W., architect
22 McCallum T. S., C.E.
23 Sleigh R., dentist
24 Wilson R., shirtmaker
24 Cheers & Smith, archts
25 Carter J. W., solicitor
26 Duckworth R., tax collector
26 Rennison E., solicitor Bolton's court
28 Knowles J. B., solictr
28 Porter B., auctioneer
28 Abbott H. J., surveyor
28 Riley B., surveyor Victoria street St. John's Church Gray Robt. A., M.D., St. John's lodge
40 Lancaster T., solicitor
39 Little E. D., solicitor
38 Cook W. A., solicitor
37 Walmsley Mrs. Eliz.
36 Waterworth E., accountant
35 Shaw J. W., solicitor
34 Chancery Office; A. Pearce, registrar
34 Talbot J., law stationer
34 Birtwistle J. T., H.M. inspector of factories
33 Riley R., solicitor
32 Lewis G. H., solicitor
31 Clough T., solicitor
31 Marsden E. & B. W., agents
30 Leeming R. E., solr

30 County Loan Co.
30 Lindon Lorino, B.S. Tacketts street Library street Turkish Baths; A. Arbury, manager Orange Hall; J. C. Hadfield, secretary Central buildings Walmsley & Yates, solicitors Briscoe & Shaw, electrical engnrs Briggs & Wolstenholme, architects Gregson R. P., photographer Richmond Chambers Heppard W., accountant Chadwick C., C.E. Simpson & Duckworth, architects Inland Revenue Office; John Jones, superintdt Porter G., solicitor Law Library and Association; G. Porter, secretary

RILEY STREET.

17 Richmond W. H., spnr
21 Smith Mr. William
27 Campbell J., spinner
45 Evans R. G., joiner (j.)
47 Hunter R., moulder
59 Counsell J., baker
67 Lassey J., watchman
73 Kay J., pensioner
75 Pickup J., painter (j.)
77 Dickinson R., joiner(j.)
81 Duckworth Mrs. J.
83aClarkson W. A., grocer
85 Brade Mr. A. E.
93 Clomson D., fitter
101 Aspin N., drawer-in
103 Stephenson W., carter
117 Holden G., clothlooker
124 Turner J., moulder
122 Lancaster J., traveller
118 Carr J., miller (j.)
116 West R., labourer
104 Holt W. H., weaver
102 Marsden J., grocer
96 Mercer Miss S. A.
92 Farrer E., joiner (j.)
90 Kenyon J., mason
88 Parker T., builder
84 McDonald A., grocer
72 Warttig C., pork btchr
68 Wilson Mrs. J., shpkpr
48 Sharples A., spinner

TOWNSHIP OF BLACKBURN, №·2599

BLACKBURN UNION.

RECEIPT.

Assessment No. *19*

3 day of *Octr* 1893.

Received from Mr. Jas Bolton the sum of One *Pounds* Seventeen *Shillings &* One 'h *Pence in respect of the Poor's Rate of the above Township, made the Thirty-first day of May, 1893, at* TWO SHILLINGS AND NINE PENCE *in the Pound, on £* 13/10/- *Assessment.*

£ 1 . 17 . 1½   *John N. Anulay* Collector.

These receipts show that between 1893 and 1908, Blackburn's rates had risen from 2s. 9d. in the pound to 4s. 2d. in the pound. This was greater than the rate of inflation and reflected the growing empire of the Corporation's responsiblity.

TOWNSHIP OF BLACKBURN.

BLACKBURN UNION.

RECEIPT NO. ....

Assessment Number.		
19	2	16	3
1681	3	1	5
1938	2	7	11
8957	1	2	2

Jany 21 1908.

Received from Mr. Jas Bolton the sum of Nine *Pounds* Seven *Shillings* Nine *Pence in respect of the Poor and Borough Rate of the above-named Township, made the Fifteenth day of May, 1908, at* FOUR SHILLINGS AND TWOPENCE *in the £ on* BUILDINGS *and other* HEREDITAMENTS *not being Agricultural Land, and at one half the said Rate on* AGRICULTURAL LAND. *Amount of Assessment £* 46

£9 . 7 . 9   C D Collector.

57

Views of Blackburn town centre from *Harmsworth's Universal Encyclopedia* of 1922.

Blackburn. Views of this busy industrial town of Lancashire. 1. The Town Hall, built in 1856. 2. The Exchange, built in 1865, a fine example of modern Gothic architecture. 3. A corner of the Blackburn Boulevards

58

CONCLUSION

Blackburn's shopping areas have been constantly changing ever since the Industrial Revolution. Every decade has seen treasured buildings torn down, and familiar paths of roads and rivers diverted, blocked or covered. As the town expanded, open gardens and moorland became built-up multi-storied shopping precincts. Whilst there is much to regret (and also to applaud) about the individual effects of that change, the change itself could not possibly have been avoided if Blackburn was to become and remain a thriving population centre. What can be controlled is the nature and timing of such changes: the forces forging the shape of Blackburn's shopping centre have been varied and sometimes volatile.

At the turn of the century, Blackburn's shopkeepers were already painfully aware of the threat to their livelihoods posed by the development and increasing accessibility of competitor towns like Preston and Manchester, and by new multiple stores. They tried to manage trade to their benefit by regulation of shop hours and days, by prosecution of unscrupulous or *'over-generous'* traders, and by positive promotions such as the Shopping Festivals of 1909 and 1913, the latter of which attracted nearly a quarter of a million visitors to Blackburn. But as early as 1910 council members were acknowledging the need for a recasting of parts of the town street plan and the construction of a new shopping centre. The first plan was advanced by Liberal councillors, and was soon answered by one from the Conservatives. However, conflict between the political groups and the commercial interests supporting them stalled any practical action. In 1923, leading citizen Thomas Ritzema proposed a more ambitious scheme to a meeting of the Chamber of Trade in the *'White Bull'*, whereby the removal of the market to the run-down area between Ainsworth Street and Penny Street was again suggested. Ritzema wanted to develop the Ribble Valley as the site of a garden city project which would be served by Blackburn. *"In two or three years' time"* he argued, *"we shall be in the midst of a big and permanent revival of trade, and by taking the tide at the flood, we should ride on to fortune"*. But the economic climate was far from favourable in the 1920s and '30s, and Ritzema's scheme remained no more than a distant aspiration for the town's dignitaries in the years leading up to the Second World War.

Public funds were hardly plentiful after 1945, either. The authorities finally covered the setts of the town centre roads with asphalt, but the old Market Hall's Superintendent celebrated its centenary in 1948 with the confident boast that, since its re-designing in 1935, *"more than a hundred deputations from local authorities*

✿ Blackburn's Great Opportunity. ✿

SCHEME FOR THE REGENERATION OF THE SHOPPING CENTRE.

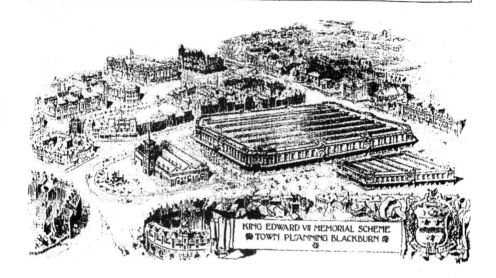

A missed opportunity? These are two versions of a proposal for the construction of new covered markets in *Ainsworth Street* presented to Blackburn's Council as early as 1910. The new centre was to be built as a memorial to King Edward VII with an 80-year loan from the government, but wars, recession and local politics meant that the transformation did not begin for another half-century.

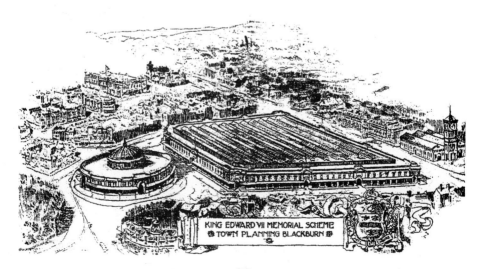

Blackburn's Market Hall and Clock Tower, landmarks of the Victorian and Edwardian town centre and now lost for a generation.

MARKET PLACE, BLACKBURN.

E.02195

61

Janry 27th 1901 0

M James Strut Chapel Members Tea Meeting

Bought of CALVERTS,

Late PICKERING,

GROCERS AND CONFECTIONERS,

53, LARKHILL, BLACKBURN.

QUALITY UNEQUALLED HARTLEY'S MARMALADE AND & TABLE JELLIES. ALWAYS RELIABLE

Plain Loaves		1	8
Brown "			8
Tea Cakes		3	6
Cracknells		1	8
Scones		1	3
Sweets		8	6
Tea		2	0
Sugar		1	8
Butter		6	3
Milk		1	0
	1	8	2

Settled with thanks
Jany 29 1910
M. E. Calvert

62

have inspected Blackburn Market Hall, and have been unanimous in their praise of the facilities of a modern, useful and artistic store". Yet the days of the old town centre were numbered. Through the 1950s it became increasingly clear that to meet the demands of modern shopping – and even more urgently, modern traffic – the plan to rehouse the market should be resuscitated, and developed to entail the rebuilding of the heart of Blackburn's shopping centre in ultra-modern style.

Even this new development was scaled down somewhat from its original 150-acre scope, and faced a barrage of criticism from indepenent traders, ratepayers and conservationists. It was the formidable partnership of councillors George Eddie and Robert Mottershead – leaders of the Labour and Conservative groups respectively – which took the redevelopment plan from the architect's table to the streets of Blackburn. A marathon public enquiry took place in Windsor Hall whilst the new market was built over the cleared site above the river Blakewater from 1962 to 1964. By 1967 Phase One of the shopping centre was open, and Phase Two was finished by 1971. When *'Debenhams'* and *'W.H.Smiths'* moved into the Third Phase of the development in 1979, Blackburn had gained a modern covered precinct of over 100 shops, eight large stores, and parking for nearly 2,000 cars. Lost in the process were the handsome and historic Thwaites Arcade, Market Hall and clock, and the patchwork of streets around them which told the onlooker so much about Blackburn's past.

Certainly the changes had their critics at the time, and many of the criticisms have gained credence since: the apparently space-age buildings came to look shabby and dated; some big-name stores left the precincts not long after the opening, and it seemed tempting to turn the clock back to the days when Blackburn had its quaint independent shops, clattering cobbled streets, welcoming inns and roomy hotels. Yet the changes were ones many Northern towns had to make at some point if they were to avoid losing trade and jobs, and which Blackburn at least made earlier and more economically than others. A town so proud of its history as Blackburn was bound to feel the wrench at such upheaval, especially since the decision – forward-thinking though it was – was so long anticipated but delayed by economic and political circumstances. Indeed, if we want to look for times when mistakes were made, we might well look at inaction before the Second World War rather than action after it. The longer we hold on to a noble past, the more painful it is to abandon it. And in any case that past is not entirely gone, as we have seen here. The shops and streets, the public buildings and boulevards of the turn of the century are still to be seen, blended in more or less successfully with the legacies of previous and subsequent generations. In a hundred years, the achievements of our own time will be at least as rare and fascinating.

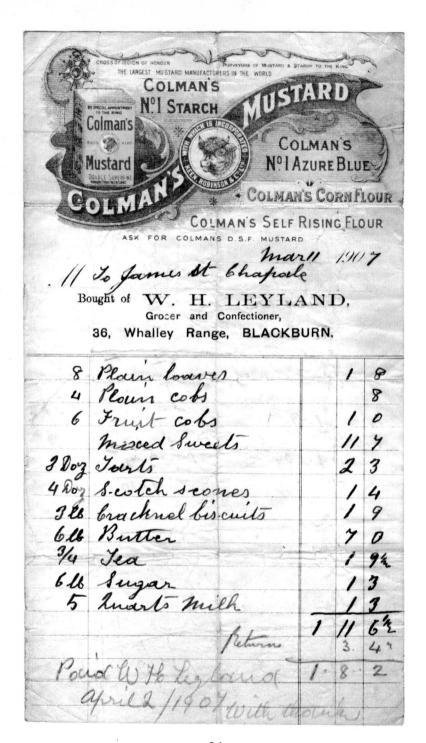

Mar 11 1907

11 To James St Chapole

Bought of **W. H. LEYLAND,**
Grocer and Confectioner,
36, Whalley Range, BLACKBURN.

		£	s	d
8	Plain loaves		1	8
4	Plain cobs			8
6	Fruit cobs		1	0
	Mixed Sweets		11	7
2 Doz	Tarts		2	3
4 Doz	Scotch scones		1	4
3 lb	Cracknel biscuits		1	9
6 lb	Butter		7	0
3/4	Tea		1	9½
6 lb	Sugar		1	3
5	Quarts milk		1	3
		1	11	6½
	Returns		3	4
		1	8	2

Paid W H Leyland
April 2 / 1907 with thanks